Revised Edition

Collins

Knowledge Lighthouse

A SKILL-BASED COURSE ON GENERAL KNOWLEDGE

2

Seema Chari
Kunal Savarkar

Components of DigiSuite

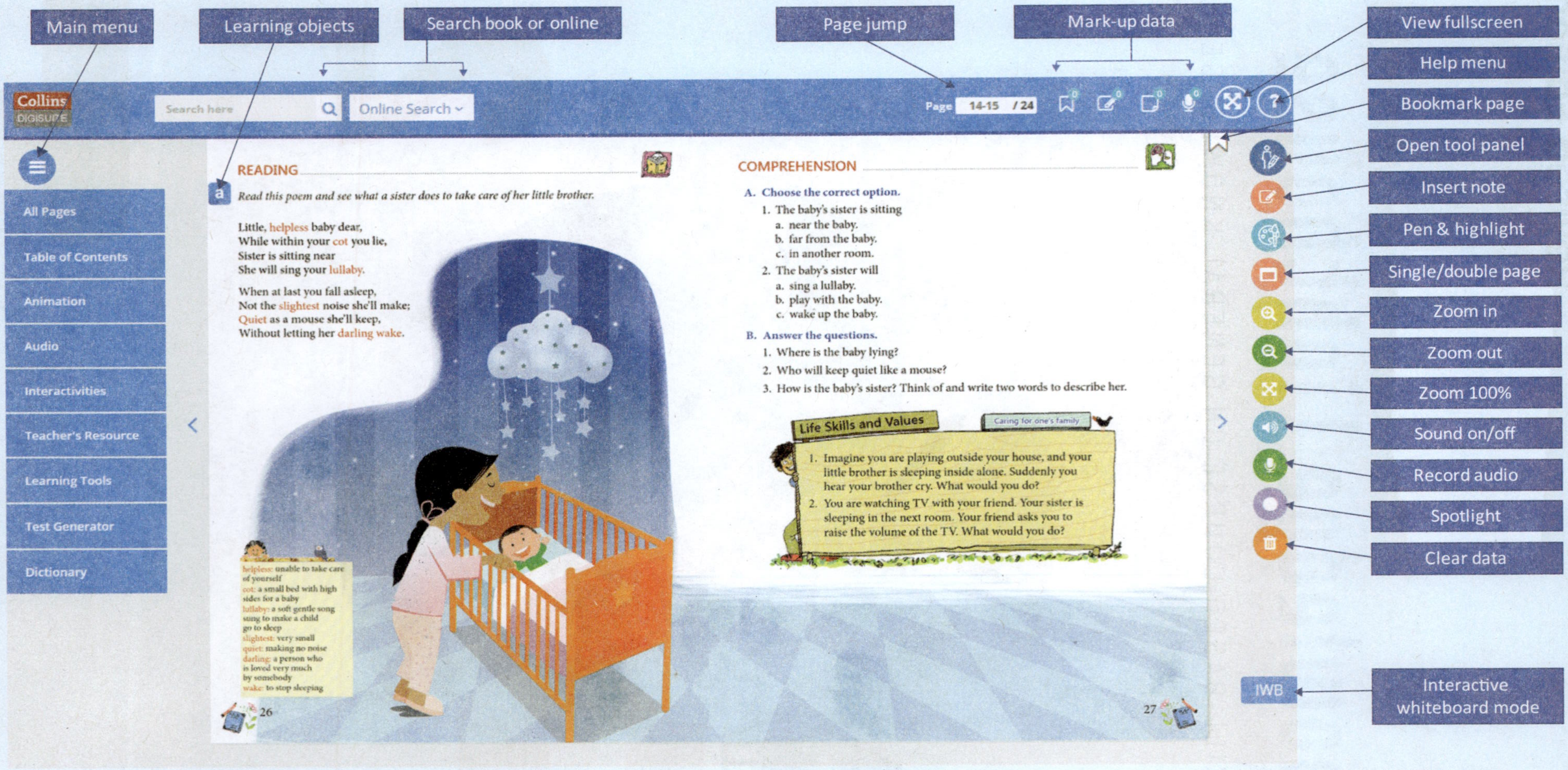

Student + Teacher			Teacher-only	
a animations	**ia** activities	**g** games	**lp** lesson plans	**tn** teacher's notes
ilt instructor-led tutorials	**w** worksheets	**v** videos	**w** worksheets	**ak** answer keys
	audio			

Preface

Like the universe, knowledge, too, is limitless. No matter how much we know, there is always more to know. In the 21st century, thanks to the leaps that technology has made and continues to make, we shall have to gather knowledge throughout our lives; so much so that we have coined a new portmanteau, to describe it: 'upskilling'.

Another novelty of the third millennium is how we access and absorb knowledge. Apart from human sources (family, teachers, friends), there are the online ones (website, social media). Yet, despite all this easy availability and accessibility, it is not always easy to distinguish between real and fake, relevant and redundant, significant and inconsequential.

Knowledge Lighthouse Revised Edition is a series meant for GenZ, that is, learners born after Y2K. The series covers 'classic' general knowledge content for learners of grades 1 to 8, but lays special emphasis on skills —learning skills, literacy skills and life skills— as well as knowledge gleaned from new learnings of the past few years, from COVID-19 to sustainability, from data science to global issues in an ever-shifting, ever-ephemeral, post-information world. All the new chapters, although dealing with topics of great gravity, are presented in an age-appropriate and friendly manner so as to kindle interest and lay the foundation for more in-depth learning.

A critical component of the Knowledge Lighthouse Revised Edition books is the India content, wherein our country in all its complexity and diversity is presented through colourful, simple and exciting tasks, plus brand-new features such as state-focus, city-focus and visit-a-monument.

A particularly career-friendly inclusion in the Knowledge Lighthouse Revised Edition series is Science, technology, engineering and mathematics (STEM), the disciplines of the future, and new global issues, presented under World Today. We hope to lighten these subjects for students, by adding a little sprinkle of trivia to them.

Sustainable development is one of the key phrases of this millennium, but what does it really mean for us, especially for children? The all-new Life on Land and Climate Action chapters not only sensitise learners but also encourage direct and immediate action.

In the Skills pages, the life skills section has tasks on safety and self-awareness. Connecting the dots is the foundation of knowledge and the series has chapters based on Higher Order Thinking Skills (HOTS) and critical thinking to train young minds to see patterns, learn to eliminate or choose details and observe better.

Become a Champion Quizzer

Knowledge Lighthouse Revised Edition encourages all learners to be curious and explore the world around them. Those who observe and absorb all the time, learn from everyone and everything; they are the ones who become quizzers. Here are six rules that will help you become a champion quizzer.

1. Be curious—look around you, see everything, read everything.
2. Listen to others.
3. Seek out new experiences.
4. Learn to link events and people.
5. Do your own research and learn to spot fake news.
6. Remember, no matter how much you know, there is much more that you have yet to learn.

Now, go for it! We are sure that this series will expose a whole new generation of learners to the fun universe of general knowledge and enhance their love for learning and discovery.

~ Seema Chari and Kunal Savarkar

In this series ...

Knowledge Lighthouse tasks are thematic and linear with visual, verbal, and strategic inputs to help students solve them and acquire knowledge through a wide range of subjects and themes.

World Around Us

16 Ways We Travel

Look at these vehicles and write their names using the words given in the help box. Write L for vehicles that move on land, W for vehicles that move on water and A for vehicles that move in the air.

1 2

World Around Us tasks take the learners on an exciting journey across the world.

Natural World

7 Baby Animals

Animals and their babies have different names. Match the babies to the

1 Calf a

2 Chick b Horse

Natural World section uncovers the magical realm of plants, animals and birds.

Life on Land

8 Clean and Green

Tick (✓) the activities that are good for the environment and cross (×) the ones that are bad.

1 Burning leaves 2 Planting trees 3 Washing clothes

Sustainable Development Goals sensitises learners towards sustainable development of the planet.

India Focus

17 Games of India

Look at the picture and write the names of the traditional games pl India using the words given in the help box.

1

India Focus tasks are created to evoke a sense of wonder and pride in our nation.

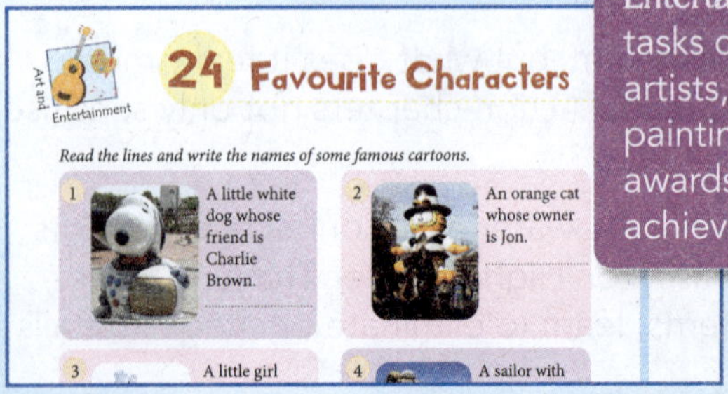
Art and Entertainment

24 Favourite Characters

Read the lines and write the names of some famous cartoons.

1 A little white dog whose friend is Charlie Brown.

2 An orange cat whose owner is Jon.

3 A little girl

4 A sailor with

Art and Entertainment tasks celebrate artists, artworks, paintings, movies, awards and achievements.

Sports

29 Sports Places

Every sport is played in a special space. Match these sports to their special spaces.

1 Cricket a Pool

Sports section provides rules and records related to different sports.

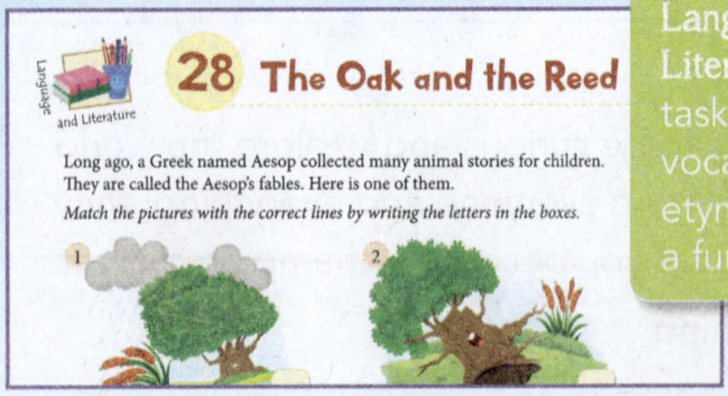
Language and Literature

28 The Oak and the Reed

Long ago, a Greek named Aesop collected many animal stories for children. They are called the Aesop's fables. Here is one of them.

Match the pictures with the correct lines by writing the letters in the boxes.

1 2

Language and Literature tasks present vocabulary and etymology in a fun way.

World Today

25 Masks and How Wear Them

Read about masks and tick (✓) the statements that are true and cr ones that are false.

1 A mask blocks the face, so the virus cannot reach others.

2 If you wear the mask, there is no need to wash your hands even if you have come home after playing in a park.

3 Children younger than 2 years old, and

Word Today introduces the learner to the COVID and post-COVID world.

Whiz fact

Walt Disney looked at many animals, like dogs, cats, frogs and horses. He finally picked a mouse and named it Mickey!

Whiz Fact is a spin-off fact about each topic or theme.

Whiz quiz

A triangle has three sides and three corners. How many sides and rectangle have?

Whiz Quiz are fun activities that encourage self-learning.

21st Century Skills

21st century skills are necessary to succeed in the Age of Information. These skills are divided into three main sets, namely, learning skills, literacy skills and life skills.

Learning Skills

- Critical Thinking and HOTS
- Creativity
- Collaboration
- Communication

Learning Skills

6 Shapes of Things

Join the dots to draw the shapes of these objects. Then write these letters for the shapes: C for circle, S for square, R for rectangle, T for triangle and O for oval.

1 2 3 5 6

Literacy Skills

- Technology
- Information
- Media
- Financial Literacy
- Data Handling

Literacy Skills

32 Animal and Bird Logos

Many companies use animals or birds in their logos.
Match these companies to their logos with the help of the clues.

	Company	Clue		Logo
1	Nestlé	Mommy bird with baby birds	a	
2	Twitter	Little bird	b	
3	Lacoste	A big animal with lots of sharp teeth	c	
4	Tripadvisor	A bird which does not sleep at night	d	

Life Skills

- Problem-solving
- Self-awareness
- Safety
- Social Skills

Life Skills

35 First Aid Kit

First aid kit is a small box containing basic medical supplies and equipment to help a sick or an injured person until full medical treatment is available. These are kept in schools, offices and malls.
Find the names of 9 things that are kept in a first aid kit from the word grid.

G	L	O	V	E	S	T	T	T	O	R	X	M	O	T
L	Q	P	H	J	C	M	O	R	P	T	R	C	V	H
O	N	J	L	A	I	E	R	T	C	H	K	R	B	E
W	P	J	M	S	S	D	C	O	O	E	M	E	R	R
E	T	H	N	T	O	I	K	R	T	R	E	A	Y	M
R	G	L	O	X	R	C	B	H	T	L	D	M	K	O
B	A	N	D	A	I	D	S	P	O	M	I	O	P	M
F	A	N	T	I	P	R	S	Q	N	O	C	E	O	E

Detailed Contents

India Focus

- Games of India
- Special Days
- India Tourism
- Indian Sportspersons

Sports

- Sports Places

Sustainable Development Goals

- Clean and Green
- Party Décor
- Gift Smart

Learning Skills

- Shapes of Things
- Lucky Seven
- Dress Up
- Colour Wheel

Literacy Skills

- Daily Activities
- Big, Bigger…
- Farm to Fork
- Animal and Bird Logos
- Computer World

Life Skills

- Our Five Senses
- The Right Words
- Play Safe
- First Aid Kit
- Find the Way

Contents

1 Words About Birds

We can describe a person or an object by comparing it with another thing. Here are some birds that are used to describe a person.

Complete the phrases with the names of the birds given in the help box. One has been done for you.

1

As happy as a lark

2

As wise as an ....

3

As gentle as a ....

4

As graceful as a ....

5

As talkative as a ....

6

As proud as a ....

Help box

dove   peacock   parrot   swan   owl

Whiz fact

The first birds were not soft and feathery. They had leathery wings and claws, and were actually dinosaurs!

Life Skills

2 Our Five Senses

SELF AWARENESS

We have five senses. We use them to see, hear, smell, taste, touch or feel.

Look at these pictures and fill in the blanks using the words given in the help box.

1

I ....

2

I ....

3

I ....

4

I ....

Help box

see hear smell taste touch feel

5

I ....

6

I ....

7

I ....

8

I ....

9

I ....

10

I ....

Whiz fact

The parts of the body, such as eyes, ears, skin, tongue and nose are called sense organs. That's how we know what is around us.

Literacy Skills

3 Daily Activities

DATA HANDLING

Be a logic detective. Here are some activities Tina does from morning till the time she comes home from school. However, they are jumbled up.

Look at the pictures and put them in the correct order by writing letters.

a

Tina reaches home. ☐

b

Tina catches the school bus in the morning. ☐

c

Tina reaches school. ☐

d

Tina gets dressed for school. ☐

e

Tina brushes her teeth. ☐

f

Tina eats breakfast.

g

Tina leaves from school.

h

Tina wakes up.

i

Tina eats lunch at home.

Whiz quiz

What did you do differently in online school? Say Y if you did the activity or N if you did not do the activity.

1 I wear a uniform.

2 I carry a tiffin.

3 I switch on my screen.

4 I mute and unmute myself.

5 I pack my bag.

6 I say and type "Present!"

7 My teacher shares her screen of activities.

8 I play with my friends in the school ground.

Life Skills

4 The Right Words

Can you find the right words to say in each of these situations?
Fill in the blanks with the right words given in the help box.

SOCIAL SKILLS

1

You sneeze.

....

2

Your classmate wins a prize.

....

3

The teacher says you are going for a picnic.

....

4

Your friend meets you in the park.

....

5

Your friend gives you a gift.

....

6

You step on your brother's foot by mistake.

....

7

Your sister is going to bed.

....

8

Your cousin wants to borrow your book.

....

Help box

yay | I am sorry | please | goodnight | congratulations | excuse me | hello | thank you

Whiz fact

The right way to behave in public is called etiquette. The word 'etiquette' was first used in France for the correct way to behave in a king's court.

Language and Literature

5 Mishmash of Words

Sometimes two words joined together form a new word. They differ by just one letter.

Using the letters given in the help box, change the blue letter in each word to get the second word. Each letter can be used only once. One has been done for you.

1 Sing-Song, a sound that keeps rising and falling.

2 Ding- ...., goes the bell.

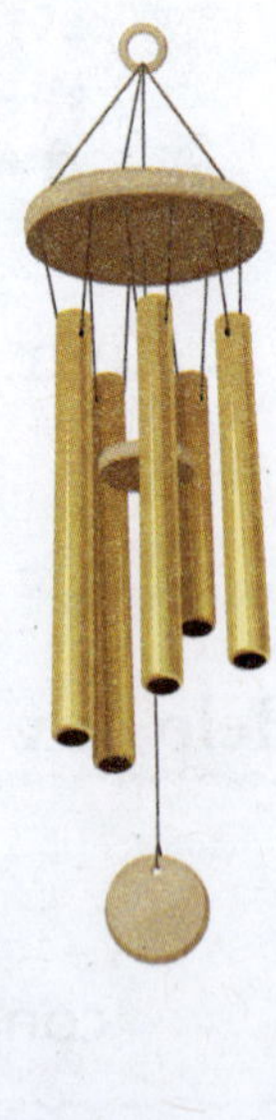

3 Knick- ...., a little thing used for decoration.

4 Tip- ...., feeling great.

5 Pitter- ...., fall the raindrops.

6 Tick- ...., goes the clock.

7 Dilly- ...., wasting time.

8 Ping- ...., we play table tennis.

9 Humpty- .... sat on a wall.

10 Zig- ...., moving left, then right, then left, then right.

Help box

a d o a o a o o a

Whiz fact

An old word that means 'nonsense' is pish-tosh.

Learning Skills

6 Shapes of Things

CREATIVITY

Join the dots to draw the shapes of these objects. Then write these letters for the shapes in the boxes given below: C for circle, S for square, R for rectangle, T for triangle and O for oval.

1

2

3

4

5

6

Whiz quiz

A triangle has three sides and three corners. How many sides and corners does a rectangle have?

7

8

9

10

11

12

13

14

Whiz fact

Pebbles on river banks are almost always oval in shape. They have no sharp edges because the flowing water makes them smooth.

Natural World

7 Baby Animals

Animals and their babies have different names. Match the babies to their parents.

1  Calf

2  Chick

3  Kitten

4  Lamb

5  Foal

a  Sheep

b  Horse

c  Hen

d  Cat

e  Cow

Whiz fact

Many baby names are made by adding -let or -ling at the end of the names of the parents. So, a baby eagle is called an eaglet. A baby goose is called a gosling and a baby duck is called a duckling.

8 Clean and Green

Tick (✓) the activities that are good for the environment and cross (×) the ones that are bad.

1

Burning leaves

2

Planting trees

3

Washing clothes in rivers

4

Leaving dustbins uncovered

5

Cycling to college

6

Cutting trees

7

Leaving the room with lights and fan switched on

8

Using cloth bags

Whiz fact

When you eat outdoors or while travelling, always carry a sheet of newspaper. You can wrap the leftovers in it and throw it in a dustbin. If the leftovers can be eaten by stray animals, do feed them. They will be so happy, and the food won't be wasted!

World Today

9 COVID Safety at School

School is not home. It is a public place. So, at school, you must do whatever is needed for you to stay safe from COVID-19.

Look at the pictures and draw 🙂 for things that must be done and draw ☹ for things that must not be done in school!

1

Making sure that classrooms are sanitized and well-ventilated.

2

Letting your masks slip to the chin or nose.

3

Wearing masks and practising social distancing during classes.

4

Shaking hands with your friends when you meet them in school.

5

Taking online classes when you are not feeling well.

6

Keeping masks on a dirty table while having your lunch.

Learning Skills

10 Lucky Seven

CRITICAL THINKING

Complete these lists. All of them have seven words. The first letter of each word has been given.

1 

Days of the Week

S ....
M ....
T ....
W ....
T ....
F ....
S ....

2 

Colours of the Rainbow

V ....
I ....
B ....
G ....
Y ....
O ....
R ....

3 

Snow White's Seven Dwarfs

D ....
G ....
H ....
D ....
S ....
B ....
S ....

4 

Musical Notes

D ....
R ....
M ....
F ....
S ....
L ....
T ....

Whiz fact

There are many more sevens. Sindbad the Sailor made seven voyages and James Bond was Agent 007.

Literacy Skills

11 Big, Bigger...

DATA HANDLING

Look at these pictures and numbers and read the lines. Then write the answers in the blank space.

1

1 millimetres

Ant

900 millimetres

Octopus

This ant's legs are .... long. This octopus' legs are .... long.

2

100 metres

Hill

2000 metres

Mountain

This hill is .... tall. This mountain is .... tall.

3

50 feet

Mango tree

80 feet

Coconut tree

The coconut tree is .... tall. The mango tree is .... tall.

4

School bag

Bucket of sand

A bucket full of sand weighs............................. My schoolbag weighs.............................

5

25 metres

15 metres

Whale

6 metres

2.8 metres

Elephant

This whale is............................tall and .... long. This elephant is ....tall and............................long.

6

10 metres

Pond

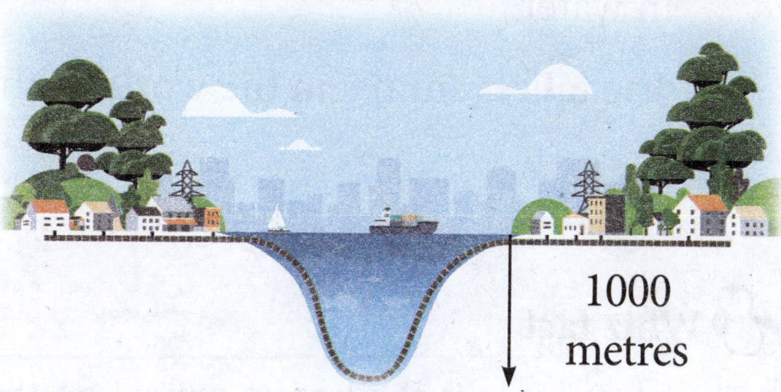

1000 metres

Sea

The pond is .... deep. The sea is .... deep.

Natural World

12 Big Animals

Write the names of some big animals in the crossword with the help of the clues.

Across

2 An animal with a hump that lives in deserts.

4 A big fish with very sharp teeth.

6 A big and heavy animal that lives near water and has legs that look like fins.

7 A furry, white animal that lives in very cold regions and eats seals and fish.

8 A large animal that hops around and carries its babies in a pocket.

10 A black, hairy animal that lives in forests and has hands like human beings.

Down

1 A big grey animal with a horn on its head.

3 A big grey animal with a long trunk and two long teeth called tusks.

5 An animal with huge mouth and short legs. It spends a lot of time in water.

9 The tallest animal in the world with a very long neck.

Whiz fact

The blue whale is the largest animal on the Earth. Its tongue is as heavy as an elephant!

Whiz quiz

Fill in the blanks.

1 .... is the fastest animal on land.

2 .... is the slowest animal on land.

Learning Skills

13 Dress Up

Four best friends are packing for vacations but their clothes are mixed up.

Use colours as clues and match the clothes and things to the friends by writing numbers. Each one should have four things to pack. One has been done for you.

CRITICAL THINKING

1

Sweater

2

Stockings

3

T-shirt

4
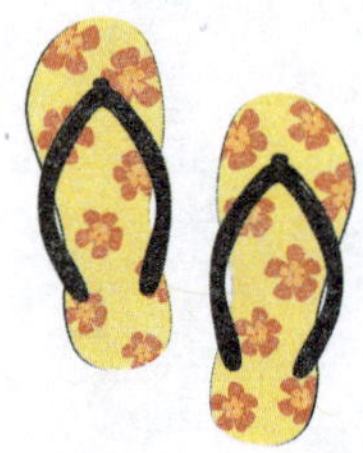
Flip flops

5

Hat

6

Sneakers

7

Cap

8

Purse

a

b

Whiz fact

If a drawer is full of red socks and green socks and you want a matching pair, how many socks should you take out without looking? You will need only three. Try it out.

9

Boots

10

Blouse

11
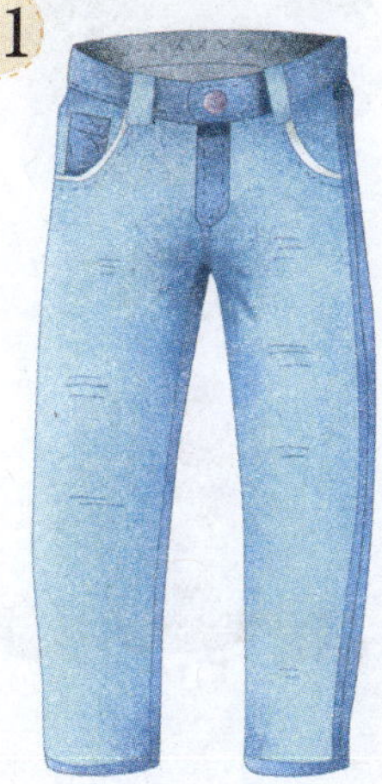
Jeans

12

Woollen trousers

13

Backpack

14

Shoes

15

Dress

c

d

16

Skirt

14 Things Used at Work

Match these people with the things they use at work.

1 Farmer 

a 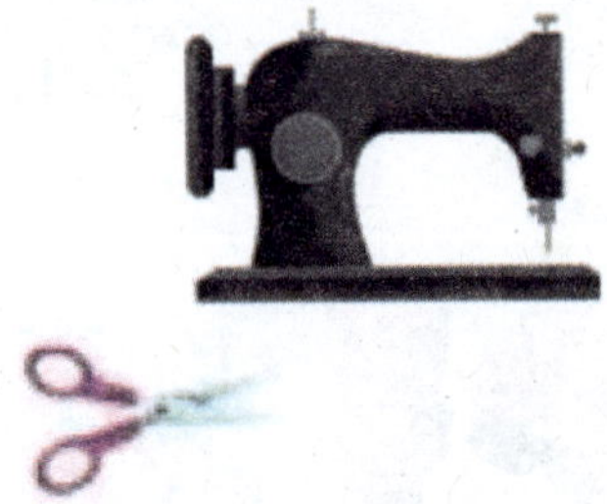

2 Cobbler 

b 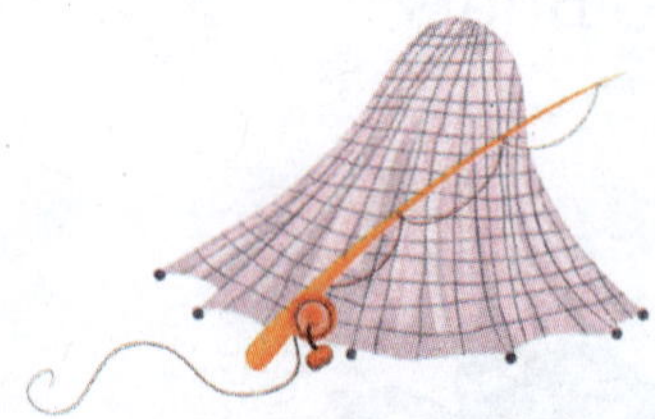

3 Baker 

c 

4 Tailor 

d 

5 Fisherman 

e 

6 Gardener

f

7 Flight attendant

g

8 Painter

h

9 Tattooist

i

10 Disc jockey

j

Whiz fact

A quizmaster needs no tools, only their brain, lots of knowledge and a list of fun questions.

Literacy Skills

15 Farm to Fork

DATA HANDLING

Let us see how things we eat are made. Write 1, 2 or 3 to put the pictures in correct sequence. One has been done for you.

a

Jam 3

Fruit 2

Plant 1

b

Milk ☐

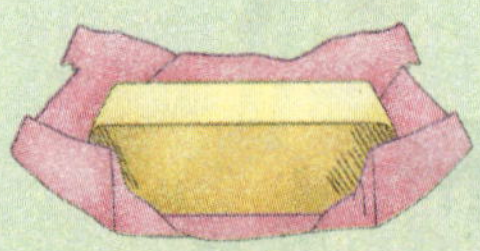

Butter ☐

Cow ☐

c

Dried leaves ☐

Tea packet ☐

Tea leaves ☐

d

Ketchup ☐

Tomato plant ☐

Tomatoes ☐

e

Honeybee ◯

Honey ◯

Beehive ◯

f

Coconut chutney ◯

Coconut tree ◯

Coconut ◯

g

Lemons ◯

Juice ◯

Lemon plant ◯

h

Chocolate ◯

Cocoa beans ◯

Cocoa tree ◯

Whiz fact

Honey never spoils if stored properly in a closed jar or a container. It can stay good for many years!

16 Ways We Travel

Look at these vehicles and write their names using the words given in the help box. Write L for vehicles that move on land, W for vehicles that move on water and A for vehicles that move in the air.

1

....

2

....

3

....

4

....

5

....

6

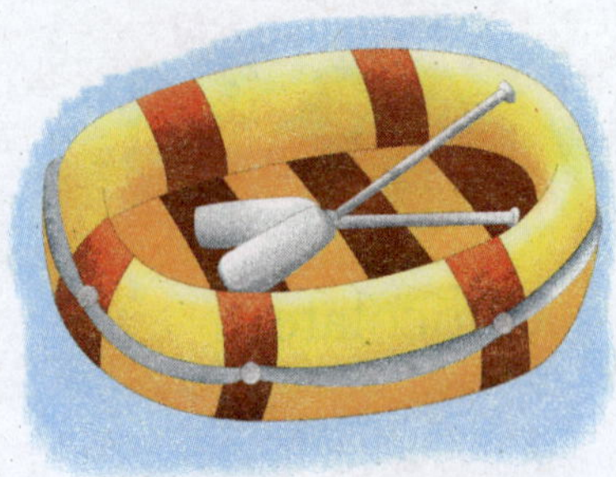

....

Whiz fact

A seaplane is an aircraft that can take off or land on water.

7

8

9

10

11

12

Help box

ship bicycle aeroplane autorickshaw train bike bus
boat scooter hot air balloon raft helicopter

Whiz quiz

Which vehicle can move underwater?

India Focus

17 Games of India

Look at the picture and write the names of the traditional games played in India using the words given in the help box.

1 ....

2 ....

3 ....

4 ....

Whiz fact

Kabaddi is one of the oldest sports in the world. It started in India and is played in all our neighbouring countries too!

5 ....

6 ....

7 ....

8 ....

Help box

hide-and-seek	*gilli danda*	skipping	seven stones
kho kho	marbles	kite flying	hopscotch

Language and Literature

18 Oh! Look at the Moon!

Some words are missing from this lovely poem about the moon. Complete the poem with the help of the pictures and the words given in the help box.

Oh! look at the moon,
She is shining up there;
Oh! Mother, she looks
Like a (1) .... in the air.

Last week she was smaller,
And shaped like a (2) ....
But now she's grown bigger,
And round as an (3) ....

Pretty moon, pretty moon,
How you shine on the (4) .... ,
And make it all bright
On my nursery (5) ....

Whiz fact

The famous poem *Twinkle, Twinkle, Little Star* was written by the poet, Jane Taylor.

You shine on my 6 .... ,
And show me their place,
And I love to look up
At your pretty bright 7 ....

And there is the 8 ....
Close by you, and maybe
That small, twinkling star
Is your little 9 ....

– Eliza Lee Cabot Follen

Help box

playthings · face · star · lamp · bow · O · door · baby · floor

Whiz activity

Using five words from the help box, write a poem of your own.

Natural World

19 Animal Homes

Write the names of the homes of our animal friends using the words given in the help box.

Horse

1 

....

2 

....

Dog

3 

....

Cow

Whiz quiz

Name two animals who build their homes.

1 ....

2 ....

Help box

kennel coop shed pen stable pond

4

Duck

....

5

Hen

....

6

Sheep

....

Whiz fact

Animals, such as cats and dogs, that live in our homes are called pets or domestic animals. Animals that live in forest are called wild animals.

20 Party Décor

A party is not a party without colourful decorations. But think for a moment– what happens to the decorations once the party is over? Sadly, they go into the bin, and end up in a landfill. Sometimes, animals and fish eat them or get caught in them and really suffer. The good news is we can decorate and reuse them without wasting.

Look at these pictures and match them with our cool décor ideas.

Picture

1. 
2. 
3. 
4. 
5. 
6. 

Décor idea

a. Decorate the cups and plates with different drawings or put your name on them

b. Make your own masks using materials like leaves, colourful paper or magazine pages.

c. Fold napkins in fun shapes and place them on the table.

d. Make your own party props with materials like thread and cardboard boxes.

e. Make your own party streamers with old newspapers, paints and ribbons.

f. Make your own twine lanterns by wrapping colourful twine over balloons, then adding glue to them. Let them dry and pop the balloon. Insert fairy lights inside each lantern and hang them in the wall.

Whiz tip

Lend your animal cutouts to your friends and have fun every birthday!

21 Food from Plants

We eat roots, stems, leaves, flowers, fruits and seeds of a plant.

Look at the pictures and complete the names of these vegetables.

1 ........AR........O........ is a root. It is long and pointy. It has thin fibres sticking out of its sides. It grows under the ground.

2 ........O........A........O is a stem. It grows under the ground. It is light brown in colour. It has black spots called 'eyes'.

3 ....AB........ ....G........ is a leaf. It is round and firm. It can have many colours like green, white or purple.

4 ........R........CC........ .... is a flower. It is green and looks like a tree with a thick trunk.

5 ....E........ .... are seeds that grow above the ground. Many can be found in a pod. Each one is round and plump and green.

Whiz fact

We can eat the stem, flower and fruit of the banana. The banana leaf is used as a plate!

India Focus

22 Special Days

We Indians celebrate or observe some special days in honour of our country and its people.

Write the dates on which we celebrate these special days using the help box.

1 

Mahatma Gandhi's birthday

....

2 

Jawaharlal Nehru's birthday

....

3 

The day India gained independence

....

4 

The day India became a republic

....

5 

A day to honour our teachers

....

Help box

15 August	2 October	26 January	5 September	14 November

Whiz quiz

Write the names of two other special days of India.

....

....

Life Skills

23 Play Safe

Draw a smiling face for actions that are safe to do in a park and a sad face for actions that are unsafe.

1

2

3

4

5

6

7

8

9

Whiz fact

If you get scratched while playing on a swing, slide or a monkey bar, you must get a tetanus injection or you might fall sick.

24 Favourite Characters

Read the lines and write the names of some famous cartoons.

1 

A little white dog whose friend is Charlie Brown.

....

2 

An orange cat whose owner is Jon.

....

3 

A little girl with bright eyes. She has adventures with her friend Boots.

....

4 

A sailor with big arms. He gets strength by eating spinach.

....

5 

A tall and funny dog, he is Mickey's best friend.

....

6 

The queen who can magically create snow.

....

Whiz fact

Walt Disney looked at many animals, like dogs, cats, frogs and horses. He finally picked a mouse and named it Mickey!

25 Masks and How to Wear Them

Read about masks and tick (✓) the statements that are true and cross (×) the ones that are false.

1. A mask blocks the face, so the virus cannot reach others. ☐
2. If you wear the mask, there is no need to wash your hands even if you have come home after playing in a park. ☐
3. Children younger than 2 years old, and anyone who can't take a mask off without help should not wear a mask. ☐
4. A mask should have more than one layer. It should not have a vent or hole. ☐
5. Masks should not cover the nose and mouth both and have gaps on the sides. ☐
6. Masks should be comfortable, so if a respirator is not comfortable, try a surgical mask, or a surgical mask with a cloth mask on top. ☐
7. There is no need to wash cloth mask often. You can even reuse disposable masks multiple times. ☐
8. Respirators can be reused a few times, but if they are dirty or damaged or do not fit snugly, throw them. ☐

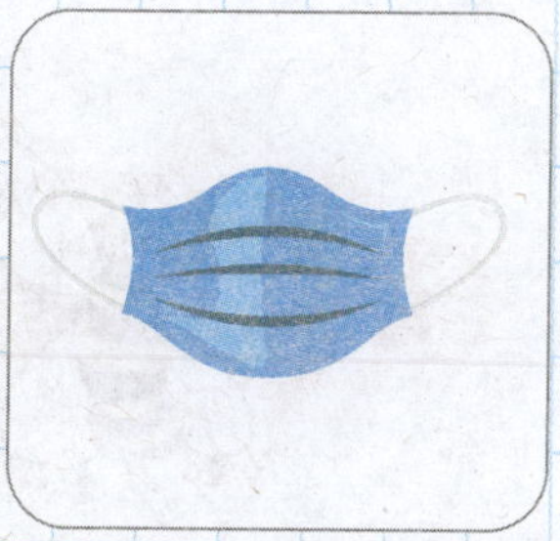

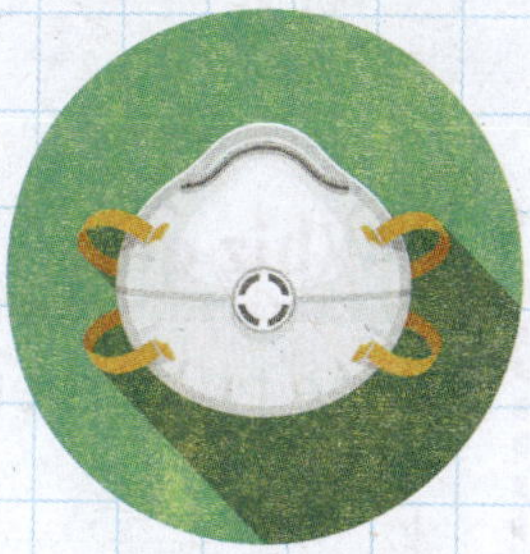

Natural World

26 Small Creatures

Read the lines about some common insects and complete their names.

1 

I have bright and colourful wings,
From flower to flower I swing!

B .... T .... E .... F .... Y

2 I am invisible, though I have mass,
I am as greeny-green as the grass.

GR .... SS .... O .... ER

3 I buzz around blooms and sip precious juice,
I make yummy honey for you!

H .... N .... B ....

4 I march and march like a soldier,
Amongst insects I am a hardworker.

A ....

Whiz quiz

Name two other insects you see in your garden.

1 ....

2 ....

5 I live in stagnant water and breed
It is on your blood that I feed!
M .... SQ .... T ....

6 My friends and I love jam and bread
Because of us greeny-grey pests, diseases spread.
HO .... S .... F ....

7 Red and black spots, I am neat as a pin
Grass and leaves, you will find me hiding in.
L .... D .... BI ....

8 I am a big insect, shiny and bright
I whizz in the garden when it is close to night.
DR .... G .... NF ....

9 Do not mess with me, I am a mean thing
If you come too close, you will get a sting!
W .... S ....

Whiz fact

Malaria, dengue and chikungunya are all deadly diseases caused by different members of the same insect group. The 5th insect on this page is the answer. Write its name here ....

27 Uniforms at Work

Many people go to work in a uniform. Look at the pictures of some working people in uniforms. Read the clues and find their names hidden in the grid. Write their names in the blanks given. One has been done for you.

1

Wears a uniform with bright, glowing stripes. Traffic police

2

Wears a khaki uniform with shiny badges and stars.

....

3

Wears a white uniform and a white cap.

....

4

Wears a space suit and a helmet.

....

5

Wears a uniform with shoulder stripes and a cap.

....

6

Wears a white coat, gloves and a mask.

....

7 

Wears a black flowing robe or a black pantsuit.

....

8 

Wears a tall hat and an apron.

....

T	R	A	F	F	I	C	P	O	L	I	C	E	D	T	N
L	I	S	O	T	R	S	I	X	P	C	H	O	I	O	U
Z	O	T	B	C	Q	M	L	A	W	Y	E	R	K	D	R
O	W	R	A	L	I	C	O	P	T	Z	F	J	L	U	S
C	G	O	S	D	O	C	T	O	R	I	A	H	A	K	E
H	A	N	N	A	U	N	U	S	R	X	K	J	Z	J	N
E	S	A	M	M	Y	O	F	X	I	C	E	R	W	N	B
T	T	U	I	E	O	U	D	O	C	R	S	E	E	C	M
R	O	T	P	O	L	I	C	E	O	F	F	I	C	E	R

Whiz fact

Some jobs do not need uniforms, only some special things. A ballet dancer wears pointe shoes and a magician wears a hat and a fancy coat.

28 The Oak and the Reed

Long ago, a Greek named Aesop collected many animal stories for children. They are called the Aesop's fables. Here is one of them.

Match the pictures with the correct lines by writing the letters in the boxes.

1 

2 

3 

4 

5 

6 

a **Oak:** Look at me, everyone, I'm a mighty oak;
I'm a big and strong and solid bloke!

Reed: I agree, dear Oak, but I'd like to say,
That I'm important too, in my own way;

b **Oak:** Ha! Ha! Ha! Look at you, puny reed,
I'm king of the woods, not a useless weed!

Reed: I'm sure you are great and big and strong;
Just don't be rude: that's mean and wrong.

c **Oak:** Pah! Silly Reed, who cares what you think?
Just one little flood, and you will simply sink!

Reed: Alright, dear Oak, if that's what you feel,
I have no problem if I bend and kneel.

d That night the wind and the rain worked up a storm
The oak and the reed closed in to stay warm.

As the lightning flashed and the thunder roared,
The reed bent and folded, and finally scored;

e The storm raged on, all through the night;
The oak struggled, but ultimately lost the fight.

The mighty oak tree, though big and strong,
Fell with a crash and a bang: it didn't last long.

f The humble reed swayed to the breeze;
So it lived long and happy, in a life of ease.

Whiz fact

A fable is a story in which animals, birds, insects or even magical creatures are used to tell the story.

29 Sports Places

Sports

Every sport is played in a special space. Match these sports to their special spaces.

1

Cricket

a

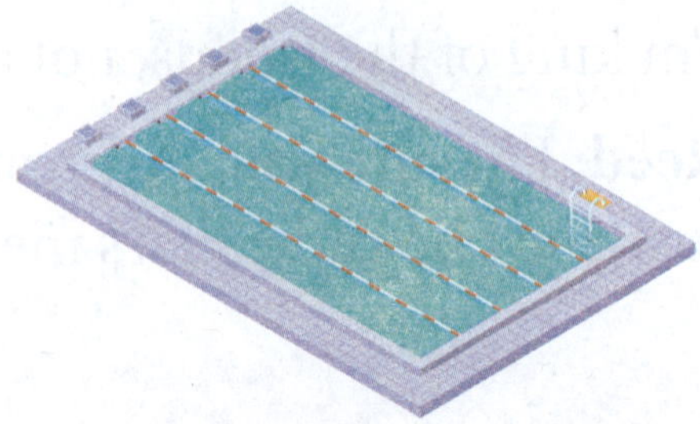

Pool

2

Football

b

Court

3

Tennis

c

Field

4

Swimming

d

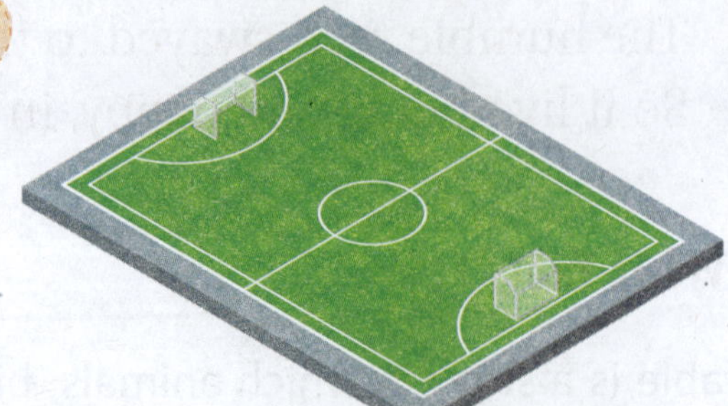

Field

5

Hockey

e

Court

6

Horse racing

f

Rink

7

Skating

g

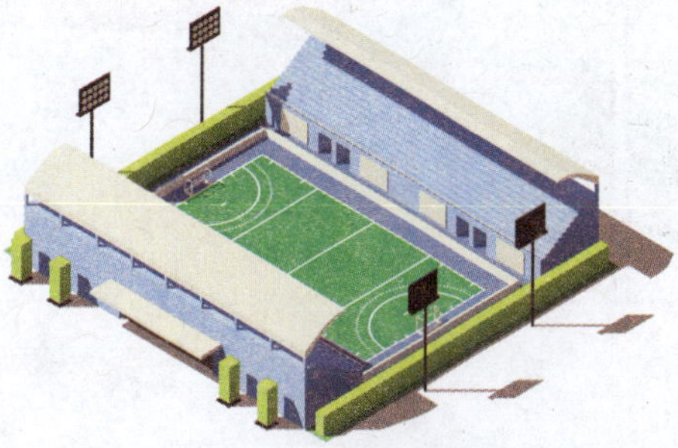

Field

8

Badminton

h

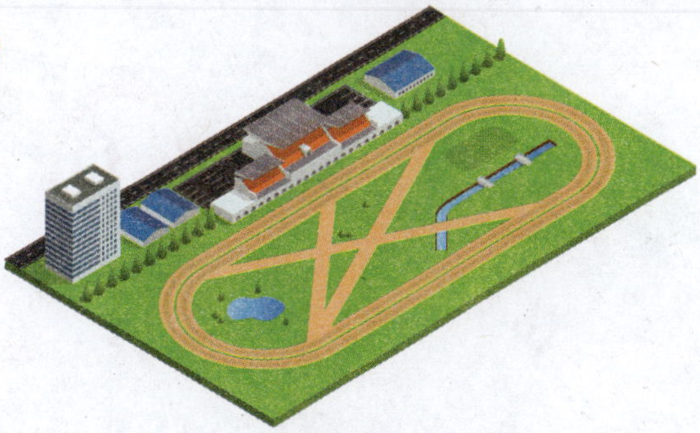

Racecourse

Whiz fact

Tennis can be played on clay, real grass or artificial grass.

30 On the Road

What do these road signs mean? Write the correct answers using the words given in the help box.

Help box

Parking — Zebra crossing — School Ahead — U-turn — Hospital — One-way

Natural World

31 Beautiful Blooms

Read the lines about some flowers and complete their names.

1

L .... T .... S is the national flower of India. It grows in ponds. It has floating leaves.

2

M .... I .... O .... D is a golden yellow or orange flower. It is used for making garlands.

3

J .... S .... I .... E is a small white flower. It has a lovely scent. It is used to make flower-strings and perfumes.

4

R .... E has a lovely scent and soft petals. It has many colours like red, pink, yellow, white, and its stems have sharp thorns.

5

O .... CH .... D is a brightly coloured flower used as decoration at weddings and other celebrations.

Whiz quiz

Name two flowers we can wear in our hair.

1 ....

2 ....

Literacy Skills

32 Animal and Bird Logos

Many companies use animals or birds in their logos.

Match these companies to their logos with the help of the clues.

Companies	Clues	Logos
1 Nestlé	Mommy bird with baby birds	a
2 Twitter	Little bird	b
3 Lacoste	A big animal with lots of sharp teeth	c
4 Tripadvisor	A bird which does not sleep at night	d
5 Metro Goldwyn Mayer	A roaring animal with a mane	e 
6 Qantas	An Australian animal whose baby is in its pocket	f

Whiz fact

An aeroplane is like a big flying bird. Many national airlines, like Japan Airlines and Singapore Airlines, have birds as their logos.

33 India Tourism

Read the lines about some of the famous buildings and monuments of India and write their names using the words given in the help box.

1 The .... has four pointy towers at four corners. It is in Hyderabad.

2 The .... is a tall red and white tower. It is in New Delhi.

3 The .... is next to the sea. It is in Mumbai.

4 The .... is covered in gold foil. It is in Amritsar.

5 The .... is made of pure white marble. It has four towers at four corners and gardens around. It is in Agra.

6 The .... has a large white dome. It is named after a Queen of England. It is in Kolkata.

7 The .... is red and white. The wind can pass through its many windows. It is in Jaipur.

8 The .... is a temple that looks like a huge chariot on wheels, pulled by horses. It is in Konark, Odisha.

Help box

Gateway of India	Charminar	Hawa Mahal	Victoria Memorial
Sun Temple	Qutub Minar	Golden Temple	Taj Mahal

Whiz fact

The India Gate in New Delhi is a memorial to the soldiers who fought bravely and lost their lives for the country.

34 Water on the Earth

Water is found in many places on the Earth.

Read the lines and write the name of the form of water using the words given in the help box.

1

Bigger than any sea

....

2

A white blanket of light flakes

....

3

A body of water flowing into the sea

....

4

A small body of water where fish and frogs live

....

5

Many streams of water falling off a cliff

....

6

Drops of water on leaves, flowers and grass

....

7

Small rocks of ice falling from the sky

....

8

A large area of fresh water, surrounded by land

....

Help box

pond, hail, snow, lake, waterfall, river, dew, ocean

Whiz fact

A large part of our Earth is covered with water. That is why Earth is called the 'blue planet'.

Life Skills

35 First Aid Kit

SAFETY

First aid kit is a small box containing basic medical supplies and equipment to help a sick or an injured person until full medical treatment is available. These are kept in schools, offices and malls.

Find the names of 9 things that are kept in a first aid kit from the word grid.

G	L	O	V	E	S	T	T	T	O	R	X	M	O	T
L	Q	P	H	J	C	M	O	R	P	T	R	C	V	H
O	N	J	L	A	I	E	R	T	C	H	K	R	B	E
W	P	J	M	S	S	D	C	O	O	E	M	E	R	R
E	T	H	N	T	O	I	K	R	T	R	E	A	Y	M
R	G	L	O	X	R	C	B	H	T	L	D	M	K	O
B	A	N	D	A	I	D	S	P	O	M	I	O	P	M
F	A	N	T	I	P	R	S	Q	N	O	C	E	O	E
S	C	I	S	S	O	R	S	W	W	T	I	G	T	T
X	P	L	A	S	S	I	R	H	O	L	N	L	R	E
B	A	D	A	G	E	O	H	X	O	A	E	A	A	R
V	O	Y	T	V	E	T	N	Q	L	N	S	S	N	O
B	A	N	D	A	G	E	O	F	E	T	U	T	T	A
R	I	V	R	X	Z	M	L	D	F	I	O	R	R	C
E	V	B	X	A	N	T	I	S	E	P	T	I	C	B

1

Cream

2

Antiseptic

3

Fork

4

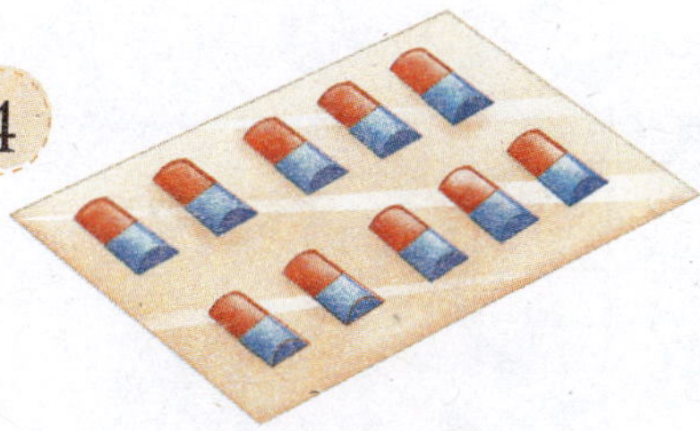

Medicines

5

Stapler

6

Cotton wool

7

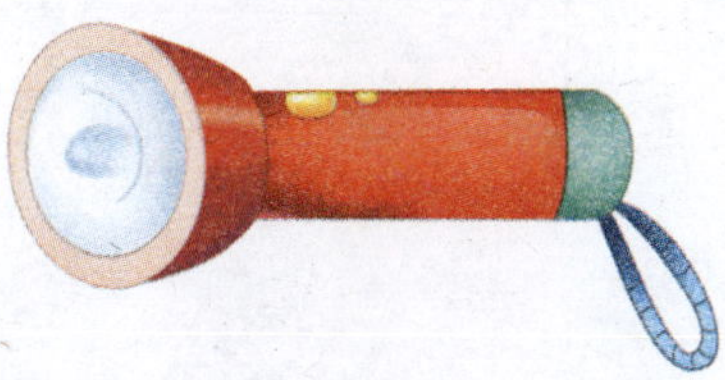

Torch

8

Scissors

9

Remote control

10

Band Aids

11

Ribbon

12

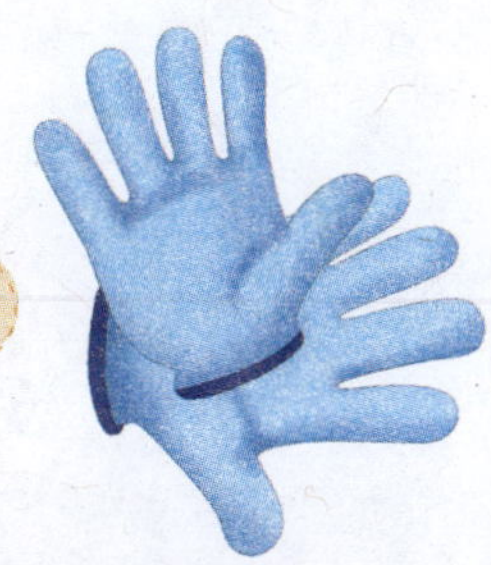

Gloves

13

Lipstick

14

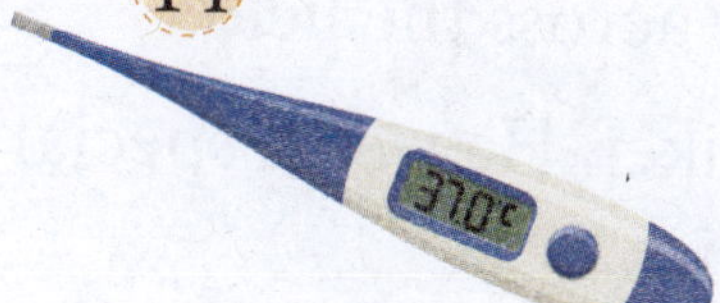

Thermometer

15

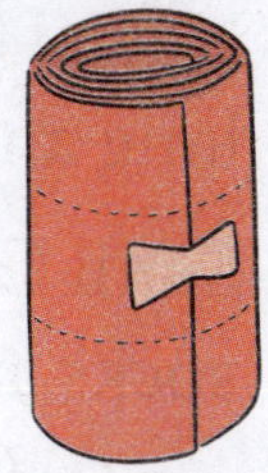

Bandage

Whiz fact

First aid kits are usually green or red with a white plus sign on them. These bright colours make it easier to find them during emergencies.

India Focus

36 Indian Sportspersons

Look at the pictures of some sportspersons from India. Read the clues and write the names of the sports they play to complete the crossword puzzle. The words in the help box will help you.

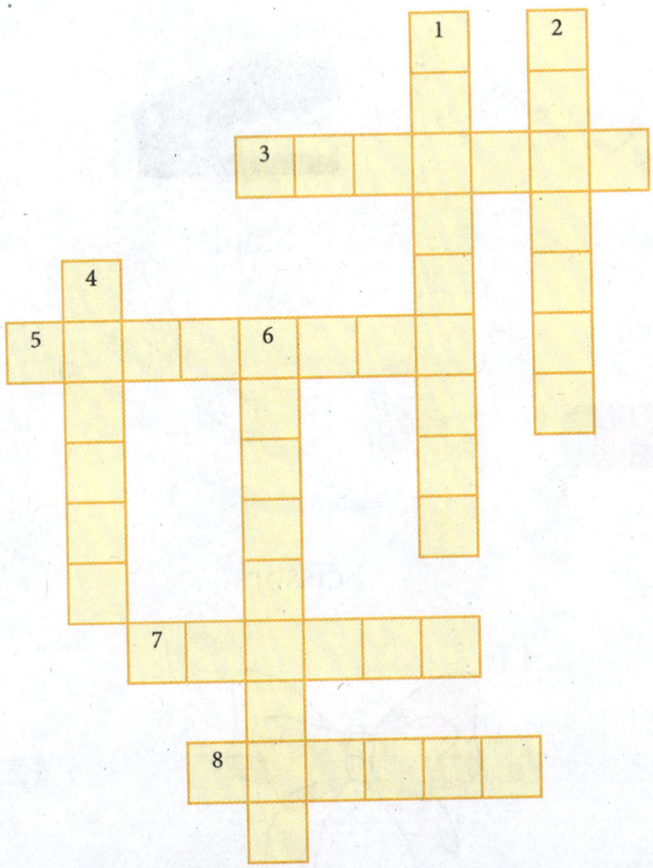

Across

3 Neeraj Chopra is an athlete. He has a very strong arm and throws a long and heavy spear across the field.

5 Sunil Chhetri is a striker. He wears special shoes called studs, knee socks and a jersey shirt.

7 Sumit Nagal has become the first Indian to win an international tournament in the COVID-19 era. He wears a t-shirt, a wristband and plays with a racquet and a ball.

8 Sardara Singh plays with a J-shaped stick and ball. He plays on a grass-covered ground called turf.

Down

1 Sakshi Malik wears a shirt called singlet, shorts and light shoes.

2 Virat Kohli is a batsman. He wears a helmet, batting pads and gloves. He plays with a bat.

4 MC Mary Kom has very strong arms. She wears gloves and punches her opponents in a space called a ring.

6 PV Sindhu wears a skirt and a shirt. She plays with a racquet and a shuttlecock.

Sardara Singh

Sumit Nagal

PV Sindhu

Sunil Chhetri

MC Mary Kom

Neeraj Chopra

Virat Kohli

Sakshi Malik

Help box

Tennis	Boxing	Badminton	Cricket
Javelin	Football	Hockey	Wrestling

Whiz fact

India's first Olympic champion was Norman Pritchard, a British athlete born in Kolkata. He won two silver medals at the 1900 Olympics.

Literacy Skills

37 Computer World

Computers are used in homes, schools and offices.

TECHNOLOGY

Write the names of parts of a computer or the type of computer. All you need to do is write the names of the things in each picture and then add or subtract letters to form new words.

1 A device used to move a cursor

M +  – H

= ....

2 A small screen bigger than a phone and smaller than a computer

 – LE +  – TER

= ....

3 A part of the computer used for typing

 + 

= ....

4 A thing used to charge a laptop or keep a computer plugged in

 + C +  – T

= ....

5 A type of computer we can carry around

 – C + 

= ....

6 A type of computer kept on a table

 + 

= ....

7 A part of the computer found inside it

 + 

= ....

8 A part of the computer on which we see pictures or text

 – EY + I +  – CH

= ....

Whiz fact

A phablet is a device that is a combination of a tablet and a phone. It is bigger than a mobile phone and smaller than a tablet.

Art and Entertainment

38 Musical Instruments

Look at these musical instruments. Some of them have strings which produce sound when plucked. Some have holes which produce sound when air is blown into them. Some have parts that produce sound when we beat them with hands or sticks.

Write pluck, blow or beat for each of these instruments.

1 I .... the sitar.

2 I .... the trumpet.

3 I .... the tabla.

4 I .... the saxophone.

5 I .... the drum.

6 I .... the veena.

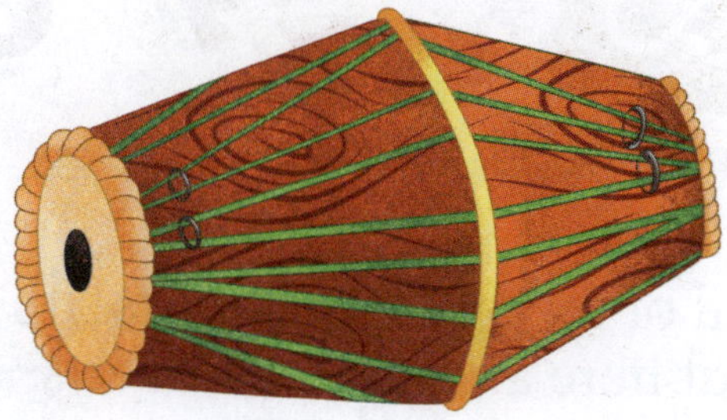

7 I .... the flute.

8 I .... the mridangam.

9 I .... the guitar.

10 I .... the shehnai.

11 I .... the kanjira.

12 I .... the sarod.

Whiz fact

The first ever musical instruments made by humans were the ones that produce sound when struck or hit. They are called percussion instruments.

39 Gift Smart

All of us love getting gifts. It's also fun choosing gifts for our friends. But here are some questions:

1. Have you loved and used all the gifts that you have received?
2. Do your friends need or want or enjoy all the gifts that they receive?

Many gifts are just used once and then thrown away. Gifts should be enjoyed, not wasted!

Match the two parts of these lines about some gifting ideas that help reduce waste in the world.

Column A

1. Tickets or vouchers so that your friend
2. A pre-loved item of clothing that your friend can wear
3. A 'promise note' offering help
4. An online gift card with which they
5. Books that be shared with friends
6. Good pencils, pen, erasers or sharpeners

Column B

a. to do their homework, clean their room or walk their dog.

b. can buy something useful that they need.

c. because it looks great and fits them perfectly!

d. after being read.

e. that can actually be used in school.

f. can enjoy a movie or a meal.

Whiz tip

Instead of wrapping paper, use newspaper. Another great idea is to use a gift bag, which can then be reused. By the way, don't write on the bag – write a note to your friend on a sheet of paper and pop it into the bag!

Learning Skills

40 Colour Wheel

Red, blue and yellow are called the primary colours. We can arrange them on a colour wheel. Mixing two primary colours gives us secondary colours.

CREATIVITY

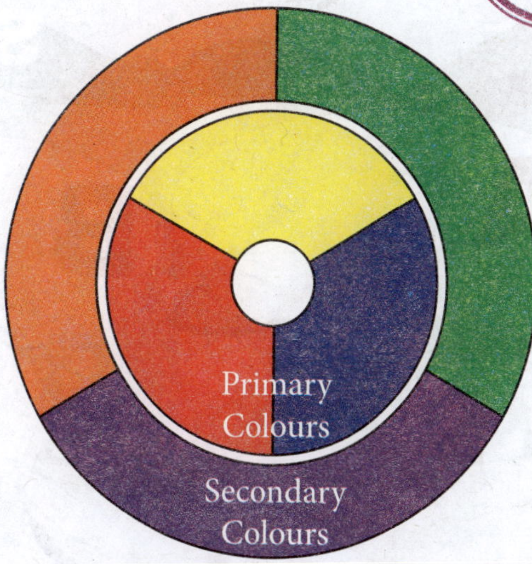

Add the colours in each part of the colour wheel and write the name of the new colour. Then colour the wheel.

1. Red + Blue = ...
2. Blue + Yellow = ...
3. Yellow + Red = ...

Life Skills

47 Find the Way

PROBLEM SOLVING

Draw lines on the paths to find out which little bear can reach the goal.

Quiz Yourself 1

Fill in the blanks. Each answer begins with a different letter of the alphabet.

1. We celebrate Independence Day on 15 ....

   a. January b. October c. August d. April

2. Red and yellow are two primary colours, the third one is ....

   a. blue b. brown c. green d. orange

3. A person who makes or repairs shoes is called a ....

   a. plumber b. tailor c. carpenter d. cobbler

4. Another word for wasting time is ....

   a. dilly-dally b. pish-tosh c. hip-hop d. pitter-patter

5. An .... is a huge grey animal with a trunk and tusks.

   a. elk b. elephant c. eagle d. enchilada

6. Cricket, football and hockey are played in a ....

   a. furrow b. farm c. field d. fold

7. .... is an old Indian sport played using sticks and stones.

   a. kho-kho b. kabaddi
   c. malkhamb d. gilli danda

8. A .... flies in the air and has a big fan on top.

   a. helicopter b. hovercraft
   c. hawk d. house fly

Quiz Yourself 2

Fill in the blanks. Each answer begins with a different letter of the alphabet.

1. A .... is to be worn on the face to protect oneself against COVID-19.

   a. sanitizer b. PPE suit c. mask d. glove

2. A .... wears a white uniform and white cap.

   a. nurse b. flight attendant c. waiter d. tattooist

3. .... is the shape of an egg.

   a. circle b. square c. triangle d. oval

4. We .... the guitar to produce sound.

   a. pluck b. blow c. hit d. slap

5. .... is a tall tower and a famous monument in Delhi.

   a. Vijay Stambh b. Qutub Minar
   c. Statue of Unity d. Hawa Mahal

6. In India, ... is celebrated on 26 January.

   a. Independence Day b. Gandhi Jayanti
   c. Republic Day d. Teachers' Day

7. .... is a white blanket of light flakes.

   a. Rain b. Hail c. Snow d. Dew

8. A person who sews clothes is called a ....

   a. tailor b. carpenter c. mason d. plumber

Quiz Yourself 3

Fill in the blanks. Each answer begins with a different letter of the alphabet.

1 We can eat an .... in a cone.

a. egg　b. orange　c. ice cream　d. apple pie

2 A lemon is squeezed to make ....

a. jam　b. juice　c. jelly　d. jalebi

3 The Sun Temple in .... looks like a huge chariot pulled by elephants.

a. Egypt　b. Konark　c. Mexico　d. Kashmir

4 The .... is India's national flower.

a. laburnum　b. lilac　c. lotus　d. lily

5 A police officer wears a khaki .... with shiny badges and stars.

a. underwear　b. ukelele　c. uniform　d. umbrella

6 A .... is a heavy and beautiful string instrument.

a. violin　b. veena　c. tabla　d. flute

7 A .... is an insect that can give us a nasty sting.

a. cockroach　b. fly　c. wasp　d. grasshopper

8 In the colour wheel, a mixture of .... and red is orange.

a. blue　b. yellow　c. green　d. white

Quiz Yourself 4

Fill in the blanks. Each answer begins with a different letter of the alphabet.

1. Moving left, right, left, right is called ....

   a. big bag b. zig zag c. rig rag d. fig fag

2. The little bright eyed girl who has adventures with Boots is called Dora the ....

   a. Adventurer b. Traveller c. Sleeper d. Explorer

3. If you step on somebody's foot by mistake, you should say ....

   a. Thank you b. Sorry c. Please d. Wow

4. The shape of a smartphone is a ....

   a. circle b. oval c. rectangle d. triangle

5. A little horse is called a ....

   a. calf b. cub c. lamb d. foal

6. It is a good idea to ride a .... instead of driving a car.

   a. cycle b. boat c. train d. aeroplane

7. A .... is a big animal with a long neck.

   a. Rhinoceros b. Hippopotamus c. Bear d. Giraffe

8. Butter is made from ....

   a. honey b. milk c. fruit d. oil

Answer Key

Page 9: 2. owl; 3. dove; 4. swan; 5. parrot; 6. peacock

Page 10-11: 1. see; 2. smell; 3. hear; 4. taste; 5. feel; 6. hear; 7. taste; 8. feel; 9. smell; 10. see

Page 12-13: 1. h; 2. e; 3. f; 4. d; 5. b; 6. c; 7. g; 8. a; 9. i

Page 14-15: 1. excuse me; 2. congratulations; 3. yay; 4. hello; 5. thank you; 6. I am sorry; 7. goodnight; 8. please

Page 16-17: 2. dong; 3. knack; 4. top; 5. patter; 6. tock; 7. dally; 8. pong; 9. dumpty; 10. zag

Page 18-19: 1. C; 2. R; 3. T; 4. S; 5. R; 6. O; 7. T; 8. R; 9. O; 10. C; 11. S; 12. S; 13. C; 14. T

Page 20: 1. e; 2. c; 3. d; 4. a; 5. b

Page 21: 1. ✗; 2. ✓; 3. ✗; 4. ✗; 5. ✓; 6. ✗ 7. ✗; 8. ✓

Page 22: 1. ☺; 2. ☹; 3. ☺; 4. ☹; 5. ☺; 6. ☹

Page 23: 1. Sunday, Monday, Tuesday, Wednesday, Thursday, Friday, Saturday; 2. violet, indigo, blue, green, yellow, orange, red; 3. Doc, Grumpy, Happy, Dopey, Sleepy, Bashful, Sneezy; 4. Do, Re, Me, Fa, So, La, Ti

Page 24-25: 1. 1 millimetres; 900 millimetres; 2. 100 metres, 2000 metres; 3. 50 feet; 80 feet; 4. 5 kg, 20 kg; 5. 15 metres, 25 metres, 2.8 metres, 6 metres; 6. 10 metres, 1000 metres

Page 26-27: Across: 2. camel; 4. shark; 6. seal; 7. polar bear; 8. kangaroo; 10. gorilla

Down: 1. rhinoceros; 3. elephant; 5. hippopotamus; 9. giraffe

Page 28-29: a. 3, 6, 11, 13; b. 2, 10, 14, 16; c. 1, 7, 9, 12; d. 4, 5, 8, 15

Page 30-31: 1. e; 2. c; 3. d; 4. a; 5. b; 6. j; 7. i; 8. g; 9. h; 10. f

Page 32-33: b. 2, 3, 1; c. 2, 3, 1; d. 3, 1, 2; e. 1, 3, 2; f. 3, 1, 2; g. 2, 3, 1; h. 3, 2, 1

Page 34-35: 1. aeroplane, A; 2. boat, W; 3. bus, L; 4. train, L; 5. bicycle, L; 6. raft, W; 7. bike, L; 8. helicopter, A; 9. scooter, L; 10. hot air balloon, A; 11. autorickshaw, L; 12. ship, W

Page 36-37: 1. kite flying; 2. gilli danda; 3. skipping; 4. marbles; 5. seven stones; 6. hide-and-seek; 7. kho kho; 8. hopscotch

Page 38-39: 1. lamp; 2. bow; 3. O; 4. door; 5. floor; 6. playthings; 7. face; 8. star; 9. baby

Page 40-41: 1. stable; 2. kennel; 3. shed; 4. pond; 5. coop; 6. pen

Page 42: 1. d; 2. c; 3. b; 4. f; 5. a; 6. e

Page 43: 1. carrot; 2. potato; 3. cabbage; 4. broccoli; 5. peas

Page 44: 1. 2 October; 2. 14 November; 3. 15 August; 4. 26 January; 5. 5 September

Page 45: 1. ☹; 2. ☺; 3. ☹; 4. ☺; 5. ☺; 6. ☹; 7. ☺; 8. ☹; 9. ☺

Page 46: 1. Snoopy; 2. Garfield; 3. Dora the Explorer; 4. Popeye; 5. Goofy; 6. Elsa

Page 47: 1. ✓; 2. ✗; 3✓; 4. ✓; 5. ✗; 6. ✓; 7. ✗; 8.✓

Page 48-49: 1. butterfly; 2. grasshopper; 3. honeybee; 4. ant; 5. mosquito; 6. housefly; 7. ladybird; 8. dragonfly; 9. wasp

Page 50-51: 2. police officer; 3. nurse; 4. astronaut; 5. pilot; 6. doctor; 7. lawyer; 8. chef

T	R	A	F	F	I	C	P	O	L	I	C	E	D	T	N
L	I	S	O	T	R	S	I	X	P	C	H	O	I	O	U
Z	O	T	B	C	Q	M	L	A	W	Y	E	R	K	D	R
O	W	R	A	L	I	C	O	P	T	Z	F	J	L	U	S
C	G	O	S	D	O	C	T	O	R	I	A	H	A	K	E
H	A	N	N	A	U	N	U	S	R	X	K	J	Z	J	N
E	S	A	M	M	Y	O	F	X	I	C	E	R	W	N	B
T	T	U	I	E	O	U	D	O	C	R	S	E	E	C	M
R	O	T	P	O	L	I	C	E	O	F	F	I	C	E	R

Page 52-53: 1. d; 2. e; 3. f; 4. a; 5. c; 6. b

Page 54-55: 1. c; 2. d; 3. b; 4. a; 5. g; 6. h; 7. f; 8. e

Page 56-57: 1. School ahead; 2. U-turn; 3. Parking; 4. Hospital; 5. Zebra crossing; 6. One-way

Page 58: 1. lotus; 2. marigold; 3. jasmine; 4. rose; 5. orchid

Page 59: 1. d; 2. f; 3. a; 4. c; 5. b; 6. e

Page 60-61: 1. Charminar; 2. Qutub Minar; 3. Gateway of India; 4. Golden Temple; 5. Taj Mahal; 6. Victoria Memorial; 7. Hawa Mahal; 8. Konark Sun Temple

Page 62-63: 1. ocean; 2. snow; 3. river; 4. pond; 5. waterfall; 6. dew; 7. hail; 8. lake

Page 64-65:

G	L	O	V	E	S	T	T	T	O	R	X	M	O	T
L	Q	P	H	J	C	M	O	R	P	T	R	C	V	H
O	N	J	L	A	I	E	R	T	C	H	K	R	B	E
W	P	J	M	S	S	D	C	O	O	E	M	E	R	R
E	T	H	N	T	O	I	K	R	T	R	E	A	Y	M
R	G	L	O	X	R	C	B	H	T	L	D	M	K	O
B	A	N	D	A	I	D	S	P	O	M	I	O	P	M
F	A	N	T	I	P	R	S	Q	N	O	C	E	O	E
S	C	I	S	S	O	R	S	W	W	T	I	G	T	T
X	P	L	A	S	S	I	R	H	O	L	N	L	R	E
B	A	D	A	G	E	O	H	X	O	A	E	A	A	R
V	O	Y	T	V	E	T	N	Q	L	N	S	S	N	O
B	A	N	D	A	G	E	O	F	E	T	U	T	T	A
R	I	V	R	X	Z	M	L	D	F	I	O	R	R	C
E	V	B	X	A	N	T	I	S	E	P	T	I	C	B

1. Cream; 2. Antiseptic; 3. Bandage; 4. Medicines; 5. Gloves; 6. Cotton wool 7. Scissors; 8. Thermometer; 9. Band Aids

Page 66-67: Across: 3. javelin; 5. football; 7. tennis; 8. hockey

Down: 1. wrestling; 2. cricket; 4. boxing; 6. badminton

Page 68-69: 1. mouse; 2. tablet; 3. keyboard; 4. power cable; 5. laptop; 6. desktop; 7. motherboard; 8. monitor

Page 70-71: 1. pluck; 2. blow; 3. beat; 4. blow; 5. beat; 6. pluck; 7. blow; 8. beat; 9. pluck; 10. blow; 12. beat; 13. pluck

Page 72: 1. f; 2. c; 3. a; 4. b; 5. d; 6. e

Page 73: 1. purple; 2. green; 3. orange

Page 74: Bear A will reach the goal

Page 75: Quiz Yourself 1:

1. c; 2. a; 3. d; 4. a; 5. b; 6. c; 7. d; 8. a

Page 76: Quiz Yourself 2:

1. c; 2. a; 3. d; 4. a; 5. b; 6. c; 7 c; 8. a

Page 77: Quiz Yourself 3:

1. c; 2. b; 3. b; 4. c; 5. c; 6. b; 7. c; 8. b

Page 78: Quiz Yourself 4:

1. b; 2. d; 3. b; 4. c; 5. d; 6. a; 7. d; 8. b